# LOS AN

## WHAT'S INSII

## MAPS

On the pages that follow, the gray numbers after place names
refer to the number of the map on which those sites can be found
and the coordinates for that location on that map.

① L.A. County

② L.A. Westside

③ Santa Monica & Venice Beach

④ Pasadena

⑤ Downtown L.A.

The Globe Pequot Press
Guilford, Connecticut

Los Angeles, sprawling over 460 square miles, is much more than the glamorous film capital of the world. It has leading-edge design and architecture, outstanding museums, vibrant cultural life, and top-class cuisine. It is also one of the United States' most ethnically diverse cities, evolving and adapting to its differing cultures with an ease that borders on rapacity. Downtown is a swirling architectural melting pot, Hollywood is buzzing with galleries and museums, while Beverly Hills, Bel-Air, and Westwood are dripping in celebrities and are home to some of the world's most expensive real estate.

3

## SIGHTS

### BEVERLY HILLS ② 4D

This once sleepy town is now the home of movie stars and has transformed itself into a glitzy glorification of conspicuous consumption. Wander through the town and, at Rodeo Drive (see p. 16), explore the extravagant shops. Take a tour above Sunset Boulevard for a glimpse of the celebrity homes and the manicured universe that is Beverly Hills, with the pink Beverly Hills Hotel (see p. 53).

### CATHEDRAL OF OUR LADY OF THE ANGELS ① 3E & ⑤

At 11 stories high, with a massive set of bronze front doors created by sculptor Robert Graham, the Roman Catholic cathedral sits atop Bunker Hill and can be seen from the Hollywood Freeway, especially at night, when the 50-foot cross is illuminated. Consecrated in 2002, it was the vision of Spanish architect Jose Rafael Moneo and was the first cathedral to be built in the United States in 30 years. :: Open Mon-Fri. 6:30 am-7 pm, Sat 9 am-7 pm, Sun 7 am-7 pm. Organ recitals Wed 12:45 pm. 555 W Temple St, Downtown, 213/680-5200, olacathedral.org

### CHINATOWN ① 1E

Ancient and modern cultures mix here, traditional food markets and shops alongside trendy art galleries and hip clubs. Established during the 1850s, when thousands of Chinese were drafted over to work on the railroads and in the local gold mines, this area is the colorful focal point of Chinese-American life in L.A.

California's number-one tourist attraction first opened in 1955 and now spreads over 185 acres. Divided into eight sections, the park deserves two days of exploration. Start your trip on Main Street, USA, and from here, step into futuristic Tomorrowland, with the highlights of Star Tours, a virtual-reality blast into space, and a high-speed tumble on Space Mountain roller coaster. Head off to meet Goofy and Donald in Mickey's Toontown before visiting the landmark Sleeping Beauty Castle in Fantasyland. Experience the Indiana Jones Adventure and take a leisurely Jungle Cruise in Adventureland. Disneyland is always crowded in summer, particularly weekends, so go early or midweek. :: Open daily. Adm. 1313 Harbor Blvd, Anaheim, 714/781-4565, disneyland.com.

### DOWNTOWN LA ① 2E & ⑤

This mixture of historic, ethnic and business districts includes El Pueblo de Los Angeles, Chinatown, the Jewelry-district and the Fashion District. Visit Grand Central Market's food hall (see p. 21) and look for the historic 1920s theaters in the Broadway Theater District, many of which now house stores. The whole area is going through massive regeneration with stunning new constructions such as the Walt Disney Concert Hall (see p. 27).

Built as a pleasure garden in the 1880s, this park covers 160 acres and contains several excellent museums, galleries, and libraries. The California Science Center is an accessible space, with an IMAX theater and a 50-ft transparent figure showing the human body. The Natural History Museum of Los Angeles County has exhibits covering dinosaurs and Native American culture. The Fisher Gallery specializes in 19th-century American art, while the pretty Rose Garden provides the perfect setting for a quiet wander

### TAKE A ROAD TRIP

The trip along Mulholland Drive (① 1A–1A) is one of the best free tours in town. The road winds for 23 miles along the spine of the Santa Monica Mountains from Hollywood down to the ocean. There are plenty of viewing spots where you can pull over and see the city in all its glory as well as its most fabulous houses.

and picnic. **California Science Center**: :: Open 10 am-5 pm daily. 700 State Dr, 323/724-3623, californiasciencecenter .org **Fisher Gallery:** Open 12 pm-5 pm Tues-Sat. Bloom Walk, 213/740-4561. **Natural History Museum:** Open 9:30 am-5 pm Mon-Fri, 10 am-5 pm Sat-Sun. Adm. 900 Exposition Blvd, 213/763-3466, nhm.org

### GAMBLE HOUSE ❶ 1F & ❹

Pasadena was a lodestar for East-coasters wanting the good life at the start of the 1900s, and the neighborhood is crammed with houses constructed in the Arts and Crafts style at that time. The Gamble House is one of the finest. It was built by Charles and Henry Greene in 1908, and its dazzling wooden interiors and wide verandahs remain untouched. :: Adm. Tours only. Open noon-3 pm Thurs-Sun. 4 Westmoreland Place, Pasadena, 626/793-3334, gamblehouse.org

### THE GETTY ❶ 2c

Perched on top of a hill in Bel-Air, and with stunning views, this widely lauded museum in a building designed by architect Richard Meier is home to the world-class collection of philanthropist J. Paul Getty, who died in 2003. The vast collection spans every conceivable period. Don't miss the incomparable Impressionist works, the hand-painted ceramics, Eastern art, and antique furniture. Ingest slowly or visit twice. Make reservations. :: Open 10 am-6 pm Tues-Sun, 10 am-9 pm Fri-Sat, closed Mon. Parking fee. 1200 Getty Center Drive, Bel-Air, 310/440-7300, getty.edu

### GETTY VILLA ❶ 2B

This Roman-style villa has undergone a massive renovation and now displays Greek, Roman and Etruscan antiquities. Outside, the gardens are a haven of tranquility, with a huge reflecting pool and a Roman medicinal garden with herbs and fruit trees. Book ahead. :: Open 10 am-5 pm Thurs-Mon. Parking fee. 17985 Pacific Coast Highway, 310/440-7300, getty.edu

### GRIFFITH PARK & OBSERVATORY ❶ 1D

This beautiful 4,100-acre preserve is the largest municipal park in the United States, donated to L.A. in 1896. Within its boundaries you will find the Observatory (see box p. 9) and the Observatory Satellite, the Planetarium, Los Angeles Zoo, the Museums of the American West and Southwest, Sunset

Ranch stables, a bird sanctuary, the Greek Theatre (see p. 27), and miles of trails and hiking with fantastic views over the sprawling city. :: Open 10 am-10 pm daily. Adm. 4730 Crystal Spring Dr, 323/913-4688, laparks.org

(see p. 27)

### HOLLYWOOD ❷ 3G & ❷ 1A
The very name of this city, the long-time center of the US's film industry, is synonymous with the movies, so it's fitting that it hosts the Oscars every year in the Kodak Theatre (see p. 27) at the Hollywood and Highland Center (see p. 18). More than 2,000 stars are honored along the Walk of Fame in the pavement of Hollywood Boulevard; and some have their hand and footprints set in front of Grauman's Chinese Theatre (see p. 29).

### HOLLYWOOD SIGN ❶ 1D
The city's most famous landmark was erected in 1923 as an advertisement for a new housing development in the hills, and originally read "Hollywoodland." It now belongs to the city and is best viewed from the Griffith Observatory (see box p. 9), Beachwood Canyon Drive (❷ 1D) or from the Hollywood and Highland Center (see p. 18). There are hiking trails in the hills all around the sign.

The best time to visit this lovely Beaux-Arts mansion and magnificent estate is spring, when the 12 acres of cacti and succulents are in vivid bloom. Other highlights include the tranquil Japanese gardens and the galleries, holding a Gutenberg Bible, Gainsborough's **Blue Boy**, and ornate French furniture. :: Adm; 1st Thurs of month free. Open noon-4:30 pm Tues-Fri, 10:30 am-4:30 pm, Sat-Sun. 1151 Oxford Rd, San Marino, 626/405-2100, huntington.org

### WALK OF FAME
The Hollywood Walk of Fame (❷ 1A-1D) starts at La Brea Avenue and stretches east along Hollywood Blvd to Gower – and it's still growing. Look for the name of your favorite star of film, television, and radio.

## JAPANESE AMERICAN NATIONAL MUSEUM ❶ 2E & ❺

Dedicated to preserving the long and complex history of Japanese immigrants in America, this museum displays moving everyday memorabilia from the internment camps of World War II and a constant round of emotionally packed changing exhibitions. :: Adm. Open 11 am-5 pm Tues-Sun, 11 am-8 pm Thurs. 369 East 1st St, Downtown, 213/625-0414, janm.org

## KNOTT'S BERRY FARM ❶ 4G

With 170 great attractions, the oldest theme park in the United States recalls a gentler time. It centers on an ersatz Wild West ghost town, which grew up around a simple diner opened in the 1940s. Today you'll find stagecoach rides, Indian trails, a saloon, Wild West stuntmen, and gold panning. Steam engines circle around the park, while another train dashes through a replica silver mine. There is also a roller coaster that loops at 55mph. :: Adm. Opens daily 10 am. 8039 Beach Blvd, Buena Park, 714/220-5200, knotts.com

## LONG BEACH ❶ 5P

This is the biggest beach town in L.A. and the home of the Queen Mary (see p. 56). The beautifully developed shoreline has residential areas, stores, restaurants, canals and even a few gondolas around the "island" community of Naples in Alamitos Bay.

## LOS ANGELES COUNTY MUSEUM OF ART ❷ 6P

Opened in 1966, LACMA extends over five buildings and, with more than 250,000 exhibits, has a spectacular catalog of international work. The fine collections of Mexican masters and American art, and the Rodins in the sculpture garden stand out. The textile collection is drawn from all over the world and features Peruvian burial shrouds and 16th-century Middle Eastern carpets. :: Adm, free 2nd Tues of month. Open noon-8 pm Mon, Tues & Thurs, noon-9 pm Fri, 11 am-8 pm Sat-Sun. 5905 Wilshire Blvd, 323/857-6000, lacma.org

## MAK CENTER FOR ART & ARCHITECTURE
**2** 4E

The MAK Center is in the Rudolf M Schindler House, which was built in 1922 and is considered the first Moderne house in L.A. It offers a year-round schedule of photography exhibitions, lectures, films, and seminars, as well as tours of local architectural high spots. There are also occasional concerts.
∷ Adm. Open 11 am-6 pm Wed-Sun, tours Sat & Sun. Free from 4-6 pm Fri. 835 N Kings Rd, West Hollywood, 323/651-1510, makcenter.com

### MALIBU **1** 2A
Malibu is a popular spot for surfers with several public beaches and excellent views of the coast from Malibu, Latigo and Corral Canyon. The beachfront homesites, first rented in 1928 for $1 per square foot per month, attracted stars like Gary Cooper. Now the rich and famous live in multimillion dollar mansions in closed-off Malibu Colony.

**GRIFFITH OBSERVATORY**

Atop Mount Hollywood (**1** 1B), this domed art deco building has been renovated and extended with new exhibition halls, and the planetarium has been upgraded with state-of-the-art digital projection. Reservations required Open noon-10 pm Tues-Fri, 10 am-10 pm Sat-Sun. Closed Mon. 4800 Western Heritage Way, 213/473-0800, griffithobs.org

### MUSEUM OF CONTEMPORARY ART
**1** 2E, **6**, **2** 4E

The magical permanent collection of contemporary art here includes works by Mark Rothko, Diane Arbus, Ellsworth Kelly, Jasper Johns, Robert Rauschenberg, and Lee Friedlander, and is housed in a building designed by Arata Isozaki. A few blocks away is the Geffen Contemporary, in an old warehouse transformed by architect Frank Gehry in 1982; it hosts traveling exhibitions. MOCA also often sponsors music and spoken word concerts on weekends.
∷ Open Mon and Fri 11 am-5 pm, Thurs 11 am-8 pm, Sat and Sun 11am-6 pm. Adm: free Thurs 5 pm-8 pm. 250 S Grand Ave, 152 N Central Ave & 8687 Melrose Ave, 213/621-1741, moca.org

### MUSEUM OF JURASSIC TECHNOLOGY
**1** 2D

An entertaining museum with some highly eccentric displays. As well as a supremely academic hoard of Jurassic items, exhibits in the seven galleries contain everything from mini designs created on the head of a pin to "trashy" exhibits from a trailer park. ∷ Donations from $3-$5. Open 2 pm-8 pm Thurs, noon-6 pm Fri-Sun. 9341 Venice Blvd, Culver City, 310/836-6131, mjt.org

### NORTON SIMON MUSEUM **1** 1F & **4**

One of the best private art collections in the world occupies a building remodeled by architect Frank Gehry. An extraordinary collection of seven centuries of European art, from the Renaissance to the 20th century,

highlights the exquisite works of Raphael, Botticelli, Rubens, Rembrandt, and Goya to the Impressionists with Manet, Monet, Van Gogh, Renoir, and Cézanne, as well as sculptures by Dégas. This oasis of western art is complemented by a strong group of sculptures from India and southeast Asia, spanning the last 2,000 years. ∷ Adm. Open noon-6 pm Wed-Mon, noon-9 pm Fri. 411 W Colorado Blvd, Pasadena, 626/449-6840, norton simon.org

### PAGE MUSEUM & LA BREA TAR PITS **2** 6F

Visit one of the oldest and largest fossil pits in the world and watch the bones being cleaned, right in the heart of the city. ∷ Adm. Open 9:30 am-5 pm Mon-Fri, 10 am-5 pm Sat-Sun. 5801 Wilshire Boulevard, 323/934-7243, tarpits.org

This downtown area showcases California's café and shopping culture at its best, particularly along Colorado Boulevard. Pasadena also boasts some of L.A.'s finest cultural treasures, including the Norton Simon Museum and the Huntington Library.

### SANTA MONICA ① 3c & ③

The closest beach to L.A., this place is quintessential California. Swimmers enjoy wide sandy beaches, cyclists and skaters fill long boardwalks, shoppers flock to the stores of Santa Monica, and kids enjoy Santa Monica Pier. Just a short stroll along the promenade is Venice.

### SUNSET STRIP & WEST HOLLYWOOD ② 3F

The renowned Sunset Strip in West Hollywood is home to most of L.A.'s nightlife with famous clubs such as the Viper Room and the House of Blues (see p. 30, 31) and the star-studded bars at the Mondrian, Sunset Towers, the Standard and Chateau Marmont hotels (see p. 53, 54). Visit Melrose Avenue (see p. 16), between Fairfax Avenue and Doheny Drive, for hip boutiques, interior design and antique stores. Around Third Street (see p. 17) look for trendy stores, cafés and boutique hotels.

### UCLA HAMMER MUSEUM ② 6A

The permanent display at the Hammer is a stunning collection of Old Masters, French Impressionists, and post-Impressionists, while the Grunwald

Center for the Graphic Arts houses a massive collection of sketches and etchings from the Renaissance to present. :: Open Tues-Wed, Fri-Sat 11 am-7 pm, Thurs 11 am-9 pm, Sun 11am-5 pm. Adm. 10899 Wilshire Blvd, Westwood, 310/443-7000, ucla.edu

### UNIVERSAL STUDIOS HOLLYWOOD ② 1G

Spread over 420 acres, Universal Studios is the world's largest theme park for TV and film. Kids love the state-of-the-art rides, which include Back to the Future and Terminator 2:3D. You can also take a backlot tour of the movie studios (see p. 50, 51), where you can see movie and TV show sets and experience a flash flood, Hollywood style. Alongside the park is Universal CityWalk, a nightlife and entertainment complex with shops, movie theaters (including a 3-D IMAX), restaurants, and venues such as BB King's Blues Club. :: Open daily. Hours vary seasonally. 100 Universal City Plaza, 800-UNIVERSAL, universalstudios.com

### VENICE ❶ 3C & ❽

Here, a couple of miles from Santa Monica, you can stop for a drink, have your palm read, and watch the bodybuilders flex their pecs at Muscle Beach. Venice's maze of canals, surrounded by residences, was created by Abbot Kinney in 1905, and the area is a beautiful place to wander and see some of the best architecture in California from the 1970s to the present, including the binocular-shaped Chiat/Day Building by Frank Gehry on Main Street.

## BEACH CULTURE

Stretching almost 100 miles from Point Dume (1 2A) in the north to Balboa (❶ 6H) in the south, the coastline of Los Angeles provides beaches to satisfy every whim. Although the beaches are great at most times of year, avoid June if possible, when oceanside towns and beaches are often shrouded in a fog known aptly as the June Gloom.

In southern California the water never really heats up and has strong currents in many places; take heed before swimming. Lifeguards in their familiar wooden huts (thank you, *Baywatch*) are stationed on all the beaches; their instructions must always be followed.

### ROMANTIC BEACHES ❶ 2A

At the northernmost of Malibu beaches, the cliffs rise up high, sheltering the sands. These tend to have rocky pools and good clean water. For a bit of peace and quiet, head off to El Matador, El Pescador, or La Piedra, all north of Point Dume.

### SURFING BEACHES

Surfing is fairly territorial, so be aware of local etiquette when visiting. Easily accessible northern beaches with generally clean water include:

**Malibu Surfrider** ❶ 2A Some of the cult surf movie *Big Wednesday* was filmed here.

**Will Rogers and Topanga** ❶ 2B

**Hermosa** ① 4D) and **Manhattan** (① 4c), the beaches south of Venice, have a lively feel to them, with volleyball nets set up on sands that are crowded on weekends and in summer. At **Redondo** ① 4D you might catch a volleyball game, surf festival, or rollerblading exhibition. The 22-mile South Bay Bicycle trail runs from here to Will Rogers. (① 3B) which also has volleyball, and a playground and swimming areas.

### WHALE WATCHING

You can see them between December and March on the southern beaches and in summer in the northerly areas. Mostly Pacific gray whales migrating can be found but blue whales have also been seen in large numbers. Plenty of boats offer whale-watching and dolphin-spotting sprees (see p. 51) and you might even get your money back if you don't get to see any.

These are also popular.

**Zuma** ① 2A This wide beach further north of Malibu has strong waves for most of the year.

**Manhattan State Beach** ① 4c The original home of the Beach Boys.

**Huntington** (① 6G) and **Hermosa** (① 4D) are popular.

Whether you are a movie star or wish you looked as if you might be, you'll find whatever your heart desires in this town obsessed with appearance and image: new designers, vintage finds, and home furnishings. The stores reflect the casually luxurious California lifestyle; Californians expect the very best but don't want to look like they tried too hard. From Beverly Hills to Pasadena, from Rodeo Drive and Beverly Hills to Glendale and Sherman Oaks, style, innovation, and money keep everything turning.

## SHOPPING AREAS

### BEVERLY HILLS ② 5E

Within a small grid of streets you will find some of L.A.'s swankiest shopping, from Gucci, Chanel, Ralph Lauren, Nike Town and Barneys (see p. 17-18), to classic local stores. Don't miss the infamous Rodeo Drive (see right).

### HOLLYWOOD ① 2D-2E

Souvenir shops touting T-shirts, baseball caps and fridge magnets dot Hollywood Boulevard. Check out the Hollywood & Highland Center (see p.18), a huge shopping and entertainment complex near Grauman's Chinese Theatre.

### MELROSE AVE ② 4G

The shops here are smart, one-off boutiques, and the bars and cafés are extremely trendy. Everything stays open late and the streets draw L.A.'s buffed and gilded youth.

### PASADENA ④

An area of well-restored eclectic architectural oddities filled with stores, movie theaters, and restaurants. On the main streets are one-of-a-kind boutiques and landmark buildings; the Paseo Colorado mall has more than 140 stores, restaurants and a multiplex theater. :: Colorado Blvd, Pasadena.

### ROBERTSON BOULEVARD ② 5C-5D

This strip of casually elegant shops includes Agnès B, Kitson and Kate Spade. Look for celebs hanging out at the Ivy restaurant or the Newsroom Café.

### RODEO DRIVE ② 2A-3B & ② 5C-5D

Shops like Chanel, Ralph Lauren and Gucci populate the palm tree-lined blocks from Santa Monica Blvd to the Regent Beverly Wilshire Hotel. The people-watching is almost as good as the window shopping. At the end Via Rodeo is a new street resembling an Italian shopping street with its very own Spanish Steps.

### THIRD STREET, WEST HOLLYWOOD ❷ 5F

Third Street is the latest hip hangout in the city, with some of the funkiest designers creating L.A.'s most original clothing and accessories, furnishings, fabrics, and household objects. It is bordered by the Beverly Center (see below) at one end with the Farmers' Market (see p. 20) and the Grove (see p. 18).

### VENICE ❶ 3C & ❸

Ocean Front Walk attracts souvenir stores selling T-shirts and sunglasses, interspersed with tarot card readers, tattoo parlors and cafés. Along Abbot Kinney Boulevard, you'll find individually designed young and trendy clothing, unique jewelry and crafts, exquisite perfumes, gifts, leather goods and homewares, cafés and restaurants.

## MALLS

L.A.'s malls stock the usual chain stores and restaurants, plus an anchoring department store or two. Each has its own distinctive style.

### BEVERLY CENTER ❷ 5E

One of L.A.'s original mall complexes. Nearly 200 shops and restaurants, including Bloomingdale's (see p. 19), Macy's (see p. 19), and the Hard Rock Café, plus MAC Cosmetics, Banana Republic and Diesel, as well as the trend-setting Traffic denim store and H&M. :: Open 10 am–9 pm Mon–Fri, 10 am–8 pm Sat, 11 am–6 pm Sun. 8500 Beverly Blvd, 310/854-0071, beverlycenter.com

### SANTA MONICA ❶ 3C & ❸

With three distinct shopping areas, you don't need to head west. Third Street Promenade is a three-block pedestrian way that's home to Zara, Banana Republic, Lush, the Apple Store, Abercrombie & Fitch and Santa Monica Place with more than 120 stores including Macy's. Opposite is a branch of Sears. The whole area is full of street performers, cafés, and movie theaters Further north, Montana Avenue is home to trendy boutiques and interior design stores. At Main Street, lots of funky clothes stores, bars and a Farmers' Market make up a thriving local scene.

GLENDALE GALLERIA ❶ 1E
The most popular mall in the Valley, with more than 250 stores and a good selection of restaurants. There is also a large branch of Neiman Marcus (see p. 20). ∷ Open 10 am-9 pm Mon-Sat, 11 am-7 pm Sun. 2148 Glendale Galleria, Glendale, 818/240-9481, glendale galleria.com

THE GROVE ❷ 3H
An outdoor mall next to the Farmers' Market (see p. 20), with top stores ringing fountains and a real streetcar running from the Farmers' Market to Nordstrom. ∷ Open 10 am-9 pm Mon-Thurs, 10 am-10 pm Fri & Sat, 11 am-8 pm Sun. 189 Grove Drive, 323/900-8080, thegrovela.com

HOLLYWOOD & HIGHLAND ❷ 3H
The vibrant heart of Hollywood and the ultimate shopping and entertainment experience, around a Golden Age movie set, is the home of the Kodak Theatre (see p. 27), stores such as Virgin Megastore and American Eagle Outfitters, plus restaurants and a hotel. You can view the Hollywood sign from the fourth floor, or check out all the names of the Oscar-winning Best Films on the ground floor columns. ∷ Open 10 am-10 pm Mon-Sat, 10 am-7 pm Sun. 6801 Hollywood Blvd, 323/467-6412, hollywoodandhighland.com

WESTFIELD SHOPPINGTOWN CENTURY CITY ❷ 6C
Part of the regeneration of 20th Century Fox's backlot, this mall has 200 stores, including Louis Vuitton, restaurants, and a multi-screen cinema. ∷ Open daily. 10250 Santa Monica Blvd, 310/277-3898, westfield.com

## BOOKSTORES

BODHI TREE ❷ 4E
From Mahayana Buddhism to Catholicism to astrology, Bodhi Tree stocks everything you need to know about spiritualism. ∷ 8585 Melrose Ave, West Hollywood, 310/659-1733, bodhitree.com

---

**SALES TAX**
The local sales tax is 8.25 percent, and it's added onto everything except groceries.

### BOOK SOUP ② 4E

This great independent bookstore hosts readings and book signings. :: 8818 Sunset Blvd, West Hollywood, 310/659-3110, booksoup.com

### HENNESSEY & INGALLS ① 2C & ③

Art, architecture, design, and photography books all stocked here. :: 214 Wilshire Boulevard, Santa Monica, 310/458-9074, hennesseyingalls.com

### STORYOPOLIS ① 1D

Everything in children's books and toys. :: 12348 Ventura Blvd, Studio City, 818/509-5600, storyopolis.com

## DEPARTMENT STORES

### BARNEYS NEW YORK ② 3B

This is style central and carries the most beautiful work of designers from the United States and abroad. Everything is always imaginatively displayed. :: 9570 Wilshire Blvd, Beverly Hills, 310/276-4400, barneys.com

### BLOOMINGDALE'S ② 6C

The great New York store in L.A. :: Beverly Center, 8500 Beverly Boulevard, 310/360-2700. Also Westfield Shoppingtown Century City. bloomingdales.com

### MACY'S ② 5E & ③

One of the oldest and largest department stores in the United States. :: Beverly Center, Century City Mall, 310/854-6655. Also at Rock Plaza, Crenshaw Plaza, Glendale Galleria, Paseo Colorado. macys.com

### NEIMAN MARCUS ❷ 3A

This Texas-born store is as stylish and manicured as the ladies who favor it; an impeccable selection of women's fashions and accessories. :: 9700 Wilshire Blvd, Beverly Hills, 310/550-5900, neimanmarcus.com

### SAKS FIFTH AVENUE ❷ 3B

A longtime favorite for luxury fashion, with very good leather, shoe, and accessory departments. :: 9600 Wilshire Blvd, Beverly Hills, 310/275-4211, saksfifthavenue.com

## DISCOUNT

### LOEHMANN'S ❷ 6E

Up to 75 percent off designer items. :: 333 S. La Cienega Blvd, West Hollywood, 310/659-0674, loehmanns.com

## FOOD MARKETS

### FARMERS' MARKET ❷ 5F

An L.A. tradition, established in 1934. You can eat in or out at the food stalls. Now connected to the Grove, L.A. (see p.18). :: Open 9 am-9 pm Mon-Fri, 9 am-8 pm Sat, 10 am-7 pm Sun, 6333 W Third Street, 323/933-9211, farmers.marketla.com

### SHIPPING THE SHOPPING

If you come from overseas, most large shops will send your purchases straight to your home address via one of the big shipping companies. Shipping helps you to avoid sales tax. Keep all receipts in case your goods are lost in transit.

### GRAND CENTRAL MARKET ⑤
For California produce, with mariachi music weekends. :: Open 9 am-6 pm daily. 317 S Broadway, Downtown, 213/624-2378, grandcentralsquare.com

## JEWELRY
### ARP ② 5F
This small group of designers sell in very select stores—a must-see for collectors of art. :: 8311½ West 3rd St, 323/653-7764.

### OK ② 5F
A mix of jewelry and objects from contemporary and vintage designers, plus an extensive collection of books that span art, design and niche topics. :: 8303 West 3rd St, 323/653-3501, okstore.la

## LINGERIE
### FREDERICK'S OF HOLLYWOOD ② 1B
The original name in showgirls' undergarments. :: 6751 Hollywood Blvd, Hollywood, 323/957-5953, fredericks.com

## SWAP MEETS
Los Angeles is known for its flea markets; they happen often and all over town, with each market being held on a certain Sunday of the month. The Rose Bowl is the biggest and even attracts visitors from Japan. Check local papers for locations.

### ROSE BOWL ① 1F
Held in Pasadena (see p. 11) on the second Sunday of the month rain or shine. Sells everything from junk to the occasional valuable bargain, with dealers and buyers from around the world exploring the stalls. Some dealers know their prices but there are deals to be found. :: Adm. Open 9 am-3 pm Second Sunday of every month. Rose Bowl Dr, Pasadena, 323/560-7469, rosebowlstadium.com

### THE MELROSE TRADING POST ② 4f

A community initiative with more than 160 dealers in antiques and collectibles every Sunday. You will find Mexican handicrafts and jewelry at reasonable prices here. The proceeds from the entrance fee go toward buying new equipment for local schools. :: Adm. Open 9 am-5 pm Sun. Fairfax High School, Fairfax & Melrose, Hollywood, 323/655-7678.

### MUSIC

#### AMOEBA ② 1c

A San Francisco-based store now in L.A. You can find everything from a number-one hit to rare vinyl.
:: 6400 W Sunset Blvd, Hollywood, 323/245-6400, amoebamusic.com

### SPECIALTY

#### PLASTICA ② 5f

Every item here, from waste baskets to address books, is plastic. Many are Japanese imports. :: 8405 W 3rd St, West Hollywood, 323/655-1051, plasticashop.com

### SURF & SKATEBOARD GEAR

#### THE BOARD GALLERY ① 3c & ③

Buy a skateboard, listen to some tunes, and check out the boarding pictures on the walls. :: 1936 Abbot Kinney Blvd, Venice, 310/450-4114.

#### HORIZONS WEST SURF SHOP ① 3c & ③

Carries everything you need to look cool catching some waves—and for relaxing afterwards. :: 2011 Main Street, Santa Monica, 310/392-1122, mainstreetsm.com/HorizonsWest

### TRAVEL GOODS

#### FLIGHT 001 ② 5f

Funky flight bags, luggage tags, laptop bags and travel goods in a store decked out like the inside of an airplane cabin. :: Open 11 am-6 pm daily. 8235 W 3rd Street, 323/966-0001, flight001.com

### VINTAGE CLOTHING

**DECADES** 2 4E

Two floors stocking the finest, and often rarest, in designer clothing in exceptional condition. The downstairs, Decades Two, has more affordable sundresses and casual wear.

:: 8214 Melrose Ave, West Hollywood, 323/655-1960.

**JET RAG** 2 4C

Affordable and fun. Don't miss the Sunday $1 clothing sales outside.

:: 825 N La Brea Ave, Hollywood, 323/939-0528.

## ENTERTAINMENT

L.A. comes alive at night. In every neighborhood, theaters, cinemas, clubs, sporting arenas, bars, and restaurants are buzzing. And the chances are higher here than anywhere else in the world that you might see a celebrity cutting teeth at a local comedy club, spot a film star at a sporting event, or dance alongside a director in a darkened rock venue. Surprisingly, given the focus on nightlife, L.A. is not a late-night town. People eat early and party early—head off home before 10:30 to get a good night's sleep.

## COMEDY

### THE COMEDY STORE ❷ 3F

This has been the place to see up-and-coming comedy acts for at least a decade. There are the occasional appearances by famous comics such as Jim Carrey or Eddie Murphy. :: Open nightly. 8433 Sunset Blvd, 323/650-6268, thecomedystore.com

### THE GROUNDLINGS ❷ 4G

This sketch-and-improv venue has been the training ground for many of the more edgier performers, including a few *Saturday Night Live* regulars and Pee Wee Herman. :: Open nightly. 7307 Melrose Ave, Hollywood, 323/934-4747, groundlings.com

### LAUGH FACTORY ❷ 3F

The top names in comedy are scheduled at this garishly venue, and comics wanting to polish up their routines frequently drop in unexpectedly. :: Open nightly. 8001 Sunset Blvd, 323/656-1336, laughfactory.com

## MUSIC, DANCE & OPERA

### MUSIC CENTER ❺

The Music Center is home to the Dorothy Chandler Pavilion, Ahmanson Theater, Mark Taper Forum and Walt Disney Concert Hall. The Dorothy Chandler Pavilion is home to the L.A. Opera, under the direction of Plácido Domingo. The Ahmanson hosts a classic selection of theater and Broadway musicals, while the Forum next door hosts more experimental work. :: 135 N Grand Ave, 213/972-7211, musiccenter.org, losangelesopera.com

### UCLA PERFORMING ARTS ❷ 5B

A venue offering instrumental, vocal, and dance performances of the highest caliber, such as Elvis Costello, Youssou N'Dour, Afro-Cuban All-Stars, and Ibrahim Ferrer. :: Prices from $15 (Sept-May). 310/825-4401, uclalive.org

ranging from Rod Stewart to Nina Simone. :: 2700 N Vermont Ave, Griffith Park, 323/665-5887, greektheatrela.com

### HOLLYWOOD BOWL 2 2H

This splendid 1920s landmark amphitheater, the summer home to the L.A. Philharmonic, conducts a hectic program ranging from Latin music and jazz to rock concerts. With the least expensive tickets priced as low as $3, it's easy for a family or large group to enjoy a concert and a picnic. Cheap last-minute tickets are usually available for major concerts. :: Jun-Sept. 2301 N Highland Ave, 323/850-2000, hollywoodbowl.com

## OSCARS

### KODAK THEATRE 2 3H

The new permanent venue for the Oscars at the Hollywood & Highland Center (see p.18) also plays host to top-level concerts by the likes of Celine Dion, Prince, and Barry Manilow. :: 6801 Hollywood Blvd, 323/308-6363, kodaktheatre.com

**WALT DISNEY CONCERT HALL 5**

This shining star at the Music Center, the home of the Los Angeles Philharmonic Orchestra and Los Angeles Master Chorale, was stunningly designed by Frank Gehry and opened in October 2003. Its acoustics are exceptional. :: Grand Ave, Downtown, 323/850-2000, laphil.org

## OUTDOOR VENUES

### FORD AMPHITHEATRE 2 2H

This intimate outdoor amphitheater plays host to both theater and music performances. :: 2580 Cahuenga Blvd E, 323/461-3673, fordamphitheatre.org

### GREEK THEATRE 1 1E

A natural open-air amphitheater holding a full schedule of rock concerts,

## THEATER

LA has a thriving theater scene, ranging from independent companies like the Evidence Room to the mainstream Geffen Playhouse. For details of what's on, check reviewplays.com

### PANTAGES THEATRE ❷ 1D

Art Deco theater and home to big musicals. :: 6233 Hollywood Blvd, 323/468-1770, pantagestheatre.com

### LA STAGE TIX

Theater listings and tickets online. Full price and half price, day of show tickets also available from LA Inc.'s Visitor Information Centers (see p. 44) in downtown Los Angeles and at Hollywood & Highland. :: 213/614-0556, lastagetix.com

## TV SHOWS

### AUDIENCES UNLIMITED ❷ 1D

Free TV show tickets are available for most popular comedies, *Jerry Springer*, *The Tonight Show with Jay Leno*, and game shows. :: Check online or booth at Universal Studios. 818/753-3470, tvtickets.com

## MOVIE THEATERS

### CINERAMA DOME ❷ 3H

This beautiful building is one of the few Cinerama theaters left. It shows contemporary blockbusters. :: 6360 W Sunset Blvd, Hollywood, 323/464-4226, arclightcinemas.com

**TICKET TIPS**

Most tickets can be purchased over the phone or online. Do be aware that some services add an often large surcharge, which can be avoided by purchasing direct.

**Good Time Tickets**
For scarce tickets 323/464-7383

**La Stage Tix**
For theater 213/614-0556, lastagetix.com

**Ticketmaster**
For concerts 213/480-3232, ticketmaster.com

### EL CAPITAN ❷ 1A

This historic 1926 cinema, owned by Disney, screens Disney films. An organist opens the shows. :: 6838 Hollywood Blvd, Hollywood, 323/467-7674, disney .go.com/disneypictures/el_capitan

### EGYPTIAN THEATRE ② 3H
Classic movies are introduced by original cast or crew in this Egyptian-temple style theater created by Grauman. :: 6712 Hollywood Blvd, 323/466-3456, americancinematheque.com

### GRAUMAN'S CHINESE THEATRE ② 3H
This famous and beautiful theater with a massive screen often hosts premieres. Go early or stay late to see the handprints of the famous outside. :: 6925 Hollywood Blvd, 323/464-8111, manntheatres.com

## MUSIC CLUBS
### Jazz, Blues & Latin
#### BABE'S & RICKEY'S INN ① 3D
With blues and jazz on the menu, this club has been kicking since 1964 and is the real deal. Call for the lineup and for Monday night's jam. Fried chicken comes with admission. :: Open Wed-Mon 6 pm-2 am. 4339 Leimert Blvd, 323/295-9112, bluesbar.com

#### BAKED POTATO ② 1F
The L.A. home of fusion jazz, this spot always has a powerful lineup. The baked potatoes on the menu come topped with all kinds of goodies. :: 3787 Cahuenga Blvd, Studio City, 818/980-1615, thebakedpotato.com

#### CATALINA BAR & GRILL ② 1C
One of the best jazz venues in the city, top-name performers are always on the bill here. Set in the heart of Holly-wood and with a tasty seafood menu, this club is a great night out. :: 6725 Sunset Blvd, Hollywood, 323/466-2210, catalinajazzclub.com

### THE CONGA ROOM ② 6G
With a hot lineup of Latin musicians, this is a must if you're into mambo, merengue, and jazz. :: Prices from $10-$50. Closed at this writing, it opens in a new location in summer 2008. congaroom.com

### THE JAZZ BAKERY ① 2D
Rival to the Catalina (see left), the Bakery is a serious place for hard-core jazz. :: 3233 Helms Ave, Culver City, 310/271-9039, jazzbakery.org

## NIGHTCLUBS

### AVALON ② 1c

In the heart of Hollywood, this mega-club has a varied program of hip-hop to rock and is a venue for live concerts. :: 1735 N Vine St, Hollywood, 323/462-8900, avalonhollywood.com

### THE ECHO ① 2e

This new eastside establishment is closer to the underground than to the velvet-rope celeb scene. Electro and Latin breaks rule the floor here; you can fill up in the restaurant and keep on dancing. :: 1822 W Sunset Blvd, Echo Park, 213/413-8200.

### THE HIGHLANDS ② 3h

Part of the new Hollywood & Highland complex (see p. 18), this opulent supper club offers two floors with dining, bars, and dance spaces. :: 6801 Hollywood Blvd, 323/461-9800, thehighlandshollywood.com

### KEYCLUB ② 4e

The sizeable Keyclub is one of the top clubs in L.A. and usually hosts headliners from the worlds of house and techno. :: 9039 Sunset Blvd, West Hollywood, 310/274-5800, keyclub.com

### ZANZIBAR ① 3c

DJs spin Latin jazz, soul, and house music in this club with an Indian/African theme, perfect for dancing or lounging. :: Open 9 pm-2 am Tues-Sun. 1301 5th St, Santa Monica, 312/451-2221, zanzibarlive.com

## ROCK & POP

### THE EL REY ② 6g

This long-standing club is now a venue for some of the biggest names in indie rock'n'pop and hosts different dance club nights. :: Prices vary. 5515 Wilshire Blvd, bet Fairfax Ave & La Brea Ave, 323/936-6400, theelrey.com

### HOUSE OF BLUES ② 3e

Don't let the theme-park décor deter you—this club provides a superior sound system and stage for some great blues and jazz acts and rock bands. :: Prices vary. 8430 Sunset Blvd, West Hollywood, 323/848-5100, hob.com

### KNITTING FACTORY ② 1A

Located in the heart of Hollywood, this is the LA outpost of the New York club, with two stages hosting punk or rock performers. :: 7021 Hollywood Blvd, Hollywood, 323/463-0204, knittingfactory.com

### LARGO ② 4F

This low-key club presents "serious" musicians who are not always *that* serious. Largo is a nice reprieve from the glitz of many other Hollywood joints. Gigs have included Beck and Fiona Apple. :: Prices from $2-$10. 432 N Fairfax Ave, bet Melrose Ave & Beverly Blvd, 323/852-1073, largo-la.com

### VIPER ROOM ② 4E

This legendary rock club, once owned by Johnny Depp, has a certain notoriety—it was nearby that River Phoenix died of a drug overdose. Now it is a venue for unknown rock acts, with the odd impromptu performance by big names. :: Over 21s only. 8852 Sunset Blvd, 310/358-1880, viperroom.com

### WHISKY A GO-GO ② 4E

The original L.A. rockers' club, where the Doors and other big-name bands first played. :: 8901 Sunset Blvd, West Hollywood, 310/652-4202, whiskyagogo.com

## SPORTS

### CYCLING & SKATING

The best areas for both cycling and in-line skating are along the beach, a 22-mile-long strand from Topanga Canyon to Palos Verde. You can also cycle in local state parks, and there are plenty of places to hire bikes and skates along the beach in Santa Monica and Venice (see below).

**PERRY'S BEACH CAFÉ AND RENTALS** ③
Eight shops along the strand between Santa Monica and Venice. Santa Monica, :: 310/372-3138, perryscafe.com

## HIKING

LA is surrounded by mountain ranges, and hills run right through the city. The Santa Monica Mountains National Recreation Area has hiking information. nps.gov/samo

### HORSEBACK RIDING

**SUNSET RANCH**

Moonlight rides, with western saddles, in Griffith Park are the specialty, and all levels of riders are welcome. A trail ride is one of the best ways to take in the stunning landscape in and around Los Angeles. :: 3400 Beachwood Dr, Hollywood, 323/469-5450, sunsetranchhollywood.com

### SKIING & SNOWBOARDING

Yes, it really is true that you can ski in the morning and swim in the ocean that same afternoon—you'll just have to drive quickly! One of the closest resorts with enough snow to make the trip worth it is Big Bear Mountain. :: For info, 909/866-4607, bigbearchamber.com

### TENNIS

Los Angeles has many public courts in parks throughout the city. :: Call the L.A. Department of Recreation and Parks for details: 818/246-5613.

## SPECTATOR SPORTS

### Baseball

**DODGER STADIUM** ➊ 2E

The L.A. Dodgers play major league baseball games here throughout the season. :: Adm. 1000 Elysian Park Ave, 866/363-4377, dodgers.com

### Basketball & Ice Hockey

**STAPLES CENTER** ➊ 2E & ➎

Home to the two L.A. men's basketball teams, the L.A. Lakers and the Clippers, as well as the women's team, the Sparks. In winter you can also catch the ice-hockey team, the Kings. :: Adm. 1111 S Figueroa St, Downtown, 213/742-7340, staplescenter.com

### Football

**L.A. AVENGERS** ➊ 2E & ➎

Los Angeles suffers from an absence of major-league football, but it gets by fine with an Arena League team, and it costs less than NFL. Apr-Jul. :: Staples Center, 310/788-7744, laavengers.com

### Horse Racing

**SANTA ANITA PARK** ➊ 1G

One of the most beautiful thoroughbred racetracks in the country pays top purses. :: Seasons run from October to mid November and December through April. 285 W Huntington Dr, 626/574-7223, santaanita.com

### Soccer

**L.A. GALAXY** ➊ 4E

The hugely popular L.A. Galaxy team plays at the Home Depot Center. :: Home Depot Center, 18400 Avalon Blvd, Carson, 1/877/342-5299, lagalaxy .com

In a city as culturally diverse as Los Angeles, there is small wonder that you can find pretty much any style of food. Whether you are after a taco from a stand in a parking lot or an expensive French meal for two, you will find no shortage of options. There are delis and diners, world-class chefs competing with each other in five-star restaurants, steakhouses, burger bars, vegetarian delights, breakfast cafés, sushi bars, dim sum eateries, pasta places, curry houses, Caribbean feasts, and bars serving up strong margaritas, and martinis. Enjoy!

## BARS

More bars are cropping up all the time in L.A.—despite the fact that people are health obsessed and addicted to their cars. From chic hotel bars like the Skybar at the Mondrian (where you'll need to be a hotel guest to get in) to hip Hollywood hangouts and groovy East Side dive bars, the people-watching here is fascinating.

Liquor is served until 1 am on weekdays and 1:30 am on weekends.

### 4100 ② 2E

Caters to a hip East Side crowd; you can lounge on oriental pillows. :: 4100 Sunset Blvd, Loz Feliz, 323/666-4460.

### DRESDEN ROOM ① 2E

A classic East Side establishment serving cocktails that hasn't changed since the 1960s. :: 1760 N Vermont Ave, Los Feliz, 323/665-4294, thedresden.com

### EL CARMEN ② 5F

Buzzing, dimly lit bar serving more than 270 types of tequila – the place for margaritas and sizzling music. :: 8138 W 3rd St, Fairfax, 323/852-1552.

### FALCON ② 3G

A natural habitat for gorgeous, trendy young things, this consists of an outdoor bar, stunning lounge, and top restaurant. :: 7213 Sunset Blvd, Hollywood, 323/850-5350, falconslair.com

### JOSEPH'S ② 1C

This Moroccan-style lounge and club in Hollywood serves tasty Greek tapas. Patio. :: 1775 N Ivar Ave, Hollywood, 323/462-8697, josephscafe.com

### THE WELL ② 2D

A swanky Hollywood bar, with a jukebox, finger food, and booths and jeans as the usual attire. :: 6255 W Sunset Blvd, Hollywood, 323/467-9355.

### YAMASHIRO ② 2G

Best at sunset, this bar in the hills offers spectacular views and a wine, sake and cocktail menu. :: 1999 N Sycamore Ave, Hollywood, 323/466-5125, yamashirorestaurant.com

---

### PRICE PER PERSON

Prices are for a three-course meal for one without alcohol.

$ = cheap (under $20)
$$ = inexpensive ($20-30)
$$$ = expensive ($30-50)
$$$$ = very expensive ($50 +)

## BURGER BARS

### BOB'S BIG BOY $ ❶ 1E
With its 1950s'-style car-hop service on weekends, this landmark is always busy. ∷ 4211 Riverside Dr, Burbank, 818/843-9334, bobs.net

### IN AND OUT $
This family-owned business makes its own burgers and fries and uses only the freshest of ingredients. ∷ Many locations, 800/786-1000, inandout.com

## CAFÉS & BREAKFAST JOINTS

### EATWELL $ ❷ 4F
Both locations are much loved by locals and thrive by serving breakfast well into the afternoon. ∷ 8252 Santa Monica Blvd at Harper, West Hollywood, 323/656-1383.

### KOKOMO CAFÉ $ ❷ 5F
This lunch counter is a good place for a cajun breakfast and coffee cake in the Farmers' Market. ∷ Farmers' Market, 6333 W 3rd at Fairfax, 323/933-0773.

### MÄNI'S BAKERY $ ❷ 5F
The place to go for soy-milk cappuccinos and dairy-free sweet pies and cakes. ∷ 519 S Fairfax Ave, 323/938-8800, manisbakery.com

## DELIS & DINERS

### BAY CITIES ITALIAN DELI $ ❸
For the best Italian sandwiches—they're often big enough to feed two. ∷ Closed Mon. 1517 Lincoln Blvd, Santa Monica, 310/395-8279, baycitiesitaliandeli.com

### DINER @ THE STANDARD $$ ❷ 3F
Good, satisfying burgers 24/7. ∷ 8300 Sunset Blvd, Hollywood, 323/650-9090.

### MILLIE'S $ ❶ 2E
A community staple, Millie's serves good home cooking and breakfast all day. ∷ 3524 Sunset Blvd, Silverlake, 323/664-0404.

### SWINGERS $ ❷ 5F
Burgers and sandwiches in a colorful setting, open from 6:30 am until 4 am. ∷ 8020 Beverly Blvd & Laurel, Hollywood, 323/653-5858.

## RESTAURANTS
### Argentinian

LALA'S $-$$ ② 4G
Grilling steak in the Argentinian tradition, this restaurant is surprisingly well-priced. Skirt steak with garlic is a specialty. Outdoor terrace. ∷ 7229 Melrose Ave, 323/934-6838. Branch at 11935 Ventura Blvd, Studio City, 818/623-4477, lalasgrill.com

### Californian

AMMO $$-$$$ ② 4H
The elegant, minimal design of this space is a good backdrop for excellent food. Both crowds and staff are beautiful. ∷ 1155 N Highland Ave, Hollywood, 323/871-2666, ammocafe.com

AXE $$-$$$ ③
Japanese and French cuisines mingle to unique effect here. The organic menu and the warmth of the space inspire people to travel across town to eat here. ∷ Closed Mon. 1009 Abbot Kinney Blvd, Venice, 310/664-9787, axerestaurant.com

CIUDAD $$$ ① 2E & ⑤
A California take on Latin cuisine from chefs Mary Sue Milliken and Susan Feniger. The food is exquisite and the venue invariably full. 445 S Figueroa St, 213/486-5171, ciudad-la.com

### Caribbean

CHA CHA CHA $$ ② 3F
A festive restaurant that serves good plantains and sangria. ∷ 7953 Santa Monica Blvd, 323/848-7700, theoriginalchachacha.com

VERSAILLES $$ ② 6E & ① 2D
This low-key Cuban mini chain has passionate fans; the pork with onions makes taste buds sing. ∷ 1415 S La Cienega Blvd, S of Pico, 310/289-0392; 10319 Venice Blvd, 310/558-3168.

### French

AOC $$$ ② 3F
This pan-Mediterranean tapas bar serves cheeses, meats and tasty entrees, but the real treat is the of fine French and California central coast wines. ∷ 8022 W 3rd St, 323/653-6359, aocwinebar.com

### CAFÉ STELLA $$-$$$ ❶ 2E
Constantly packed, this hole-in-the-wall serves bistro fare with a lively vibe. ∷ 3932 W Sunset Blvd at Sanborn, Silverlake, 323/666-0265.

### LES DEUX CAFÉ $$$$ ❷ 1B
This swish red and gold restaurant is a mainstay for stylish L.A. – and the rich French food is pretty good, too. Occupies an old bungalow and courtyard. ∷ 1638 Las Palmas Ave, Hollywood, 323/462-7674, lesdeuxhollywood.com

### THE LITTLE DOOR $$$ ❷ 5F
Excellent traditional food in a lush setting. The glamorous crowd feels like St-Tropez. ∷ 8164 W 3rd St, Beverly Hills, 323/951-1210.

### LUCQUES $$$-$$$$ ❷ 4E
Chef Suzanne Goin puts a modern touch on traditional French fare. ∷ 8474 Melrose Ave, West Hollywood, 323/655-6277, lucques.com

## Indian
### ELECTRIC LOTUS $$ ❶ 2E
Good saags and curries while DJs spin bangra. ∷ 4656 Franklin Ave, Los Feliz, 323/953-0040, electriclotus.com

## Italian
### ABBOT'S PIZZA $ ❸
Pizza made with a thin crust and fresh vegetables. ∷ 1407 Abbot Kinney Blvd & California, Venice, 310/396-7334.

### CHEAP TIP
Special discounted lunch menus are often available, especially in restaurants near movie studios.

### NO SMOKING
Smoking is not allowed in restaurants or bars. If you smoke, ask if the outside seating area allows smoking as well—if not you may be out on the street.

### AL GELATO $$ ② 5E

Known for its homemade ice cream and pies; most people forget to look at the pasta dishes, which are just as good. :: Cash only. 806 S Robertson Blvd, Beverly Hills, 310/659-8069.

### LA DOLCE VITA $$$ ② 3A

Most people outside Beverly Hills don't know this place, although it has been the haunt of celebrities and California politicians for years. :: 9785 Little Santa Monica Blvd, Beverly Hills, 310/278-1845, ladolcevitabeverlyhills.com

## Japanese

### HIROZEN $$ ② 5E

A quiet, minimalist sushi bar with good fish at reasonable prices. :: 8385 Beverly Blvd, Beverly Hills, 323/653-0470, hirozen.com

### ITA-CHO $$$ ② 5G

Ita-cho serves simple Japanese dishes, including large plates of sashimi, in a minimalist dining room. Reservations on the weekend. :: 7311 Beverly Blvd, Beverly Hills, 323/938-9009.

### R-23 $$-$$$ ① 2E

Elegantly displayed sushi arrives on a plate the length of your table as you sit in sculpted cardboard chairs at this Japanese restaurant and gallery. :: 923 E 3rd St, Downtown, 213/687-7178, r23.com

### SHABU SHABU $-$$ ⑤

The menu is *shabu shabu*—thin slices of beef, vegetables, and noodles that you cook yourself. :: 127 Japanese Village Plaza Mall, bet San Pedro & Center, 213/680-3890.

## Mexican

### BORDER GRILL $$$ ③

The people from Ciudad have created California's ode to fine Mexican food. Great tequila selection. :: 1445 4th St, Santa Monica, 310/451-1655, bordergrill.com

### MEXICO CITY $$ ① 2E

A hip East Side hangout that serves good food and mean margaritas. :: 2121 Hillhurst Ave, Los Feliz, 323/661-7227.

## Spanish & Tapas

**COBRAS & MATADORS** **\$\$** **2** **5F**
The first one was so good that they had to create another one on the East Side of town. These Spanish tapas joints serve traditional fare, cheese, octopus, and patatas. The Beverly Boulevard branch is BYOB. :: 4655 Hollywood Blvd, 323 669 3922. Branch: 7615 W Beverly Blvd, 323/932-6178

## Steakhouses

**CHEZ JAY** **\$\$** **3**
This small longtime favorite is always packed, so call ahead for reservations. You never know who will be sitting in the next booth. :: 1657 Ocean Ave, Santa Monica, 310/395-1741, chezjays.com

## Vegan

**INAKA** **\$\$** **2** **5G**
Organic Japanese food that is as flavorsome as it is healthy. :: 131 S La Brea Ave, La Brea, 323/936-9353.

### CHOOSE YOUR CHEFS
Wolfgang Puck (Spago), Suzanne Goin (Lucques), Mary Sue Milliken and Susan Feniger (Ciudad) are just a few of the fine chefs working culinary miracles on L.A.'s trendy restaurant scene.

### TIPS ON TIPPING
Gratuities are not included on bills but it is customary to tip between 15 and 20 percent. It is also customary to tip \$1 per cocktail at the bar, slightly less for beer.

## PRACTICAL INFORMATION

Sprawling across 467 square miles, through mountains, back down to the lowlands, and then out to the ocean, L.A. is truly the city of the car. The network of freeways is well-defined—in fact, it is rare to see anyone on foot in the heart of the city. Most visitors rent cars on arrival, but an efficient bus system and new subway system have made navigating this vast city without a car somewhat easier. The following chapter will give you the information you need to make your trip a success.

## VISITOR INFORMATION

**BEVERLY HILLS VISITORS BUREAU** 2 5D
:: Open Mon-Fri 8:30 am-5 pm. 239 S Beverly Drive, Beverly Hills, 310/248-1015, 800/345-2210, beverlyhillsbehere.com

**LONG BEACH VISITORS CENTER** 1 5F
:: Open Mon-Fri 8 am-5 pm. One World Trade Center, 3rd Floor, Long Beach, 562/436-3645, 800/452-7829, visitlongbeach.com

**LOS ANGELES VISITORS CENTER**
**Downtown** 5
:: Open Mon-Fri 9 am-5 pm. 685 S Figueroa Street, Los Angeles, 213/689-8822, 800/228-2452, lacvb.com

**Hollywood** 2 1B
:: Open 10 am-10 pm Mon-Sat, 10 am-7 pm Sun. Hollywood & Highland Complex, 6801 Hollywood Blvd, 323/467-6412, lacvb.com

**MARINA DEL REY VISITORS CENTER** 1 3C
:: Open daily 9 am-4 pm. 4701 Admiralty Way, Marina del Rey, 310/305-9545, visitthemarina.com

**PASADENA CONVENTION & VISITORS BUREAU** 4
:: Open Mon-Fri 8 am-5 pm, 10 am-4 pm Sat. 171 South Los Robles Ave, Pasadena, 626/795-9311, 800/307-7977, pasadenacal.com

**SANTA MONICA WALK-IN VISITOR INFORMATION CENTER** 3
Also has two iMacs for Internet access.
:: Open 9 am-6 pm daily. 1920 Main Street, 310/393-7593, 800/544-5319, sant amonicacvb.com

**WEST HOLLYWOOD CONVENTION & VISITORS BUREAU** 2 4E
:: Open Mon-Fri 9 am-5 pm. 8687 Melrose Avenue, West Hollywood, 310/289-2525, 800/368-6020, visitwesthollywood.com

---

**HOLLYWOOD PASS**
This value-for-money pass includes the Starline Tours of celebrity homes, the Red Line walking tour of Hollywood (see p. 51), the Hollywood Wax Museum and either a behind-the-scenes tour of the Kodak Theatre (see p. 27) or the Hollywood Museum. Buy online or from the above locations. citypass.com

## AIRPORTS

LAX, the international airport, is 15 miles from downtown. The other airports support domestic flights.

**BOB HOPE (BURBANK) AIRPORT** ❶ 1D
The nearest airport to Hollywood.
:: 2627 N Hollywood Way, Burbank, 818/840-8840, bobhopeairport.com

**JOHN WAYNE AIRPORT** ❶ 6H
:: 18601 Airport Way, Santa Ana, 949/252-5200, ocair.com

**LAX** ❶ 3D
:: 1 World Way, 310/646-5252, lawa.org/lax

**LONG BEACH AIRPORT** ❶ 4F
4100 Donald Douglas Dr, 562/570-2600, lgb.org

**ONTARIO AIRPORT** ❶ 2H
1940 E Moore Way, Ontario, 909/937-2700 lawa.org/ont

## ARRIVING IN TOWN

Rental cars or shuttle buses are recommended to get into town, as train destinations are limited and cabs are expensive.

## By Shuttle Bus

**SUPERSHUTTLE**
:: 24-hour service. 310/782-6600, supershuttle.com

**AIRPORT SHUTTLE**
Bus service from Anaheim to airports. 800/828-6699, graylineanaheim.com

**PRIME TIME SHUTTLE**
:: 800/RED-VANS, primetimeshuttle .com

## By Taxi

Taxis stand outside the arrivals halls of all airports. If you want to pay by credit card, check to make sure the driver takes plastic. The set fare between Downtown and LAX is $42, Hollywood $50, and Malibu around $65. :: taxicabsla.org

## CAR RENTAL

**ALAMO**
:: 800/327-9633, al amo.com

**AVIS**
:: 800/331-1212, avis.com

**BUDGET**
:: 800/527-0700, drivebudget.com

**DOLLAR**
:: 800/800-4000, dollar.com

**ENTERPRISE**
:: 800/736-8222, enterprise.com

**HERTZ**
:: 800/654-3131, hertz.com

**NATIONAL**
:: 800/227-7368, nationalcar.com

### Getting a Good Deal

Always compare prices before you book. Local companies sometimes offer used car rentals that cost less than the national companies.

**BEVERLY HILLS RENT-A-CAR**
:: 800/479-5996, bhrentacar.com

**RENT-A-WRECK**
:: 800/995-0994, rentawreck.com

## PARKING

Most stores, restaurants, and institutions provide validated parking (discounted or free) to customers as well as valet parking (full service, fee parking). Street parking is also available in most areas—but watch parking signs so that you don't get a ticket.

## PUBLIC TRANSPORT

Although the car is king in Los Angeles, a decent public transport system is run within the city by the Metropolitan Transportation Authority (MTA): 800/266-6883.

### Fares and Passes

An MTA Metro Day Pass costs $3. Buy on buses and at stations for all-day travel. A flat fare for one-way is $1.25, and a transfer costs $0.25. Fares for other bus services range from $0.25 to $1.25 and hours vary from 6 am until midnight.

## Metrorail 1
The subway system consists of four lines all centering on downtown. Hours of operation are 5 am to 11 pm daily. mta.net

**The Red Line** connects the sights of downtown, going through mid-Wilshire into Hollywood, and ending in the San Fernando Valley.

**The Blue Line** runs north and south from downtown L.A. to Long Beach.

**The Green Line** runs east and west from Norwalk to Redondo Beach.

**The Gold Line** runs to Pasadena, connecting with the Red Line at Union Station.

## Buses
Various bus companies function within the area.

### BIG BLUE BUS
The **Big Blue Bus** operates on the West Side of town. The **Tide Shuttle** runs in Santa Monica from Third Street Promenade to Main Street stopping at hotels along the way. :: Santa Monica, 310/451-5444, bigbluebus.com

### CULVER CITY BUS LINES
Culver City offers its own buses with six different lines. :: 310/253-6510, ci.culver-city.ca.us

### DASH
Downtown Area Short Hop runs six lines throughout Hollywood, Mid-Wilshire, and downtown. 213/626-4455 or 310/808-2273, ladottransit.com

### MTA
Metro runs more than 200 buses throughout Los Angeles. **Metro Rapid** buses (red) run express with limited stops and are denoted with a three-figure number starting with a 7 (720, for instance, runs the length of Wilshire Boulevard from Santa Monica to downtown). **Metro Local** buses are orange. Both buses are included in the Metro Day Pass (see p. 46). :: 800/266-6883, mta.net

## Taxis
It is not common practice to stand on the street and hail a cab in L.A. Nor will you find a taxi stand anywhere. If you need a cab, you must telephone for one to pick you up. Charges are an initial $1.90 to $2.50 and then $1.60 per mile. Because the city covers such

a vast area, fares can mount quickly. If you have a group, an alternative is to hire a car or limousine service, which generally charges by the hour, with a minimum charge. Extensive listings can be found in the phone book.

## CLIMATE

They say there are two seasons in Los Angeles, 'green' and 'brown,' but you may notice more subtle changes. Temperatures vary depending on where you are; the beach is cooler, Hollywood adds 10 degrees, and the valley and Pasadena another 10.

**December to March:** These are the rainy months, when the city accumulates its entire annual rainfall. Temperatures in winter typically stay around the 60s Fahrenheit (15 to 20 Celsius) during the day and can drop at night to the 40s Fahrenheit (4 or 5 Celsius).

**April to October:** As temperatures start to rise in early April, the city blooms. During summer and into early October, temperatures during the day climb into the 90s Fahrenheit (32 Celsius); evenings can feel chilly even if it drops to the 70s Fahrenheit (20 Celsius).

## CONSULATES

**AUSTRALIAN CONSULATE** ① 6C & ① 2C
:: 2029 Century Park E, 31st Floor, Los Angeles, 310/229-4800, usa.embassy.gov.au

**BRITISH CONSULATE** ① 2C
:: 11766 Wilshire Blvd, Suite 1200, Los Angeles, 310/481-0031, britainusa.com/la/

**HONORARY CONSUL OF IRELAND** ① 2E
:: 1631 Beverly Blvd, Los Angeles, 714/374-8962

**SOUTH AFRICAN CONSULATE** ① 2D & ② 6F
:: 6300 Wilshire Blvd, Ste 600, Los Angeles, 323/651-0902

## FOR FOLKS WITH DISABILITIES

Since 1982, Los Angeles has ensured that all new buildings include access for people with disabilities. All MTA trains and buses provide access; preferred parking permits and reduced admission to some state parks can be obtained.

**CITY DEPT ON DISABILITY** ① 2E & ⑤
333 S Spring St, 213/485-6334, lacity.org/DOD/

## ELECTRICITY & VOLTAGE

US standard is AC 110 volts/60 cycles, with a plug of two flat pins set parallel to one another.

## EMERGENCY

**Emergency Number**
911 for police, fire, and ambulance.

## INTERNET

Santa Monica Walk-In Visitor Information Center (see p. 44) has two iMacs offering Internet access.

## Wi-Fi

Most libraries, bookstores, luxury hotels and coffee chains offer wi-fi access to travelers. There may be a charge.

**PERSHING SQUARE, DOWNTOWN L.A.**
Offers free wi-fi access.
:: experiencela.com

## LOST PROPERTY

**LOS ANGELES POLICE DEPARTMENT**
Notify the LAPD on the non-emergency line. :: 1-877/275-5273, lapdonline.org

**SANTA MONICA POLICE DEPARTMENT**
:: 333 Olympic Dr, Santa Monica. Substations on 1443 2nd St Santa Monica Pier, 310/395-9931, santamonicapd.org

## MAIL

US domestic letters cost $.41 and postcards $.26. To international destinations, letters cost $0.90 and postcards $.75. You can also buy stamps from vending machines in drugstores.
:: Post offices are generally open 9 am to 5 pm weekdays, 9 am to 12 pm Sat. 800/275-8777, usps.com

## MONEY

Most banks are open 9 to 5 weekdays, and until 3 Saturdays. Most shops and restaurants accept cash, travelers' checks, and credit cards. You can withdraw cash from ATMs with most cards. Money can be changed at banks, which give the best rates.

## PHARMACY

Pharmacies can be found throughout the city. :: Call 800/748-3243 (RiteAid), 800/746-7287 (CVS), or 800/925-4733 (Walgreen's).

## TELEPHONES

Local calls from pay phones are $.50 and up, depending on how long the call lasts and how far away you're calling. There are many area codes within the city, so you will often need to dial the number 1, followed by all 10 figures in the phone number, to be connected. Phone cards are widely available and get you the best rates. They're also the most convenient, since many calls are apt to cost more than $.50.

### Directory Assistance

Local directory inquiries 411. International directory inquiries 00. International calls 011 plus the country code.

## PUBLIC HOLIDAYS

Major public holidays include the following days:

| | |
|---|---|
| 1 Jan | New Year's Day |
| 3rd Mon Jan | Martin Luther King Jr Day |
| 3rd Mon Feb | Presidents' Day |
| Last Mon May | Memorial Day |
| Jul 4 | Independence Day |
| 1st Mon Sept | Labor Day |
| 4th Thur Nov | Thanksgiving Day |
| Dec 25 | Christmas Day |

## STUDIOS

### NBC TELEVISION NETWORK ❶ 1D

For the *Tonight Show with Jay Leno*, tickets are available by mail. Also a 70-minute walking tour. :: Tours 9 am-3 pm Mon-Fri. 3000 W Al ameda Avenue, Burbank, 818/840-3537, nbc.com

### PARAMOUNT STUDIOS ❶ 2D

Two-hour guided tours behind the scenes. Minimum age 12. :: Tours 10 am or 2 pm weekdays. Reservations required. 5555 Melrose Ave, Hollywood, 323/956-1777, paramount.com

### SONY PICTURES (FORMERLY MGM) ❶ 2D

Two-hour walking tour of what used to be MGM. Minimum age 12. :: Mon-Fri Reservations required. 10202 W Washington Boulevard, Culver City 323/520-8687, sonypicturesstudios.com

### UNIVERSAL STUDIOS ② 1D
The largest studio in the world (see p. 11). Give yourself a full day to take in everything. :: 100 Universal City Plaza, Universal City, 800/864-8377, universalstudios.com

### WARNER BROS. STUDIOS ① 1D
The two-hour cart tour is said to be the best backlot studio tour. Minimum age 8. Reservations recommended and photo ID required. :: Adm. Tickets may be bought online. Tours 8:30 am-4 pm Mon-Fri, later in summer. 4301 W Olive Avenue, 818/846-1403 wbstudiotour.com

## TOURS

### HOLLYWOOD TOURS
See the city, or where the stars live, shop, and hang out in L.A.'s secluded hills and on Beverly Hills' stately streets, or take the Movie Stars Tour, which finishes with a visit to Universal Studios (see p. 11). :: 800/789-9575, hollywoodtours.us

### RED LINE WALKING TOURS ② 1B
See inside Hollywood's beautiful theaters and the Stella Adler Academy with the hourly popular Hollywood Behind-the-Scenes walking tours. Also offers the Hollywood Movie Stars tour, behind the scenes at Sony Pictures. The downtown tour takes you to the Bradbury Building (see p. 57), inside some of the 1920s theaters, and through Grand Central Market (see p. 21) or to see some of its more contemporary architecture. :: 6773 Hollywood Blvd, 323/402-1074, redlinetours.com

### STARLINE TOURS OF HOLLYWOOD
See the homes of Nicholas Cage, Michael and Catherine, Tom Kat, and Barbra Streisand. Other tours include Disneyland (see p. 55), and Universal Studios (see p. 12), all in the comfort of an air-conditioned minibus. :: 323/463-3333, starlinetours.com

### WHALE WATCHING CRUISES
Take a 2½ hour trip to see the Pacific gray whales, blue whales, dolphins, seals, and others along the Californian coastline. Reservations not required. :: Rainbow Harbor, 100 Aquarium Way, Long Beach, 562/432-4900, 2seewhales.com

Los Angels has a huge variety of places to stay, from lavish resorts and traditional towers to lush, stylish getaways on the beach. Budgeteers do not want for options, either.

## LUXURY HOTELS

### BEVERLY HILLS HOTEL $$$-$$$$ ② 4c

🍽 ⅋ 𝐘 ♨ @ 🏋 ✳ Ⓟ

The "Pink Palace" has been an icon since 1912. The bedrooms are sound-proofed and there are 12 acres of landscaped gardens. The Polo Lounge is a favorite haunt of Hollywood celebrities. :: 9641 Sunset Blvd, Beverly Hills, 310/276-2251, beverlyhillshotel.com

### SUNSET TOWER $$$-$$$$ ② 3F

🍽 ⅋ 𝐘 ♨ @ 🏋 ✳ Ⓟ

This Art Deco hotel is stunning, with fantastic views of the city, especially from the wonderful roof-top pool. Rooms include Egyptian cotton linens, floor-to-ceiling windows and iPod docking stations. :: 8358 Sunset Blvd, West Hollywood, 323/654-7100, sunset towerhotel.com

## SANTA MONICA HOTELS

### FAIRMONT MIRAMAR SANTA MONICA

### $$-$$$ ③

🍽 ⅋ 𝐘 ♨ @ 🏋 ✳ Ⓟ

Built around a 100-year-old banyan tree, this hotel is in a quiet spot at the end of the Third Street Promenade (see p. 17). Some rooms and suites have ocean views. Staff are exceptionally friendly. Pool and spa. :: 101 Wilshire Blvd, Santa Monica, 310/576-7777, 800/257-7544, fairmont.com/santa monica/

| HOTELS | |
|---|---|
| 🍽 | Room service |
| ⅋ | Restaurant |
| 𝐘 | Bar |
| ♨ | Rooms with bath |
| @ | Business center |
| 🏋 | Health club |
| ✳ | Air conditioning |
| Ⓟ | Parking |

**PRICE GUIDE PER ROOM**

| | |
|---|---|
| $ | Budget (under $100) |
| $$ | Moderate ($100-$150) |
| $$$ | Expensive ($150-$250) |
| $$$$ | Deluxe ($250 +) |

### SHUTTERS ON THE BEACH $$-$$$ ❸

🕸 🍴 🍸 🛏 @ ☀ ❄ ℗

This lovely inn is right on the beach and each bedroom has a balcony overlooking the sand. Settle on a sofa in the bar and let the first-rate staff take your order. :: 1 Pico Blvd, Santa Monica, 310/458-0030, 800/334-9000, shuttersonthebeach.com

### STYLISH HOTELS AVALON $$-$$$ ❷ 6D

🕸 🍴 🍸 🛏 @ ☀ ❄ ℗

In its previous incarnation as the Beverly Carlton, Marilyn Monroe was a regular at this beautifully designed 84-room hotel. It provides everything from Frette linens to Nintendo consoles. The blue-on-blue restaurant shimmers at night around the pool. :: 9400 W Olympic Blvd, Beverly Hills, 310/277-5221, 800/670-6183 in the United States, avalonbeverlyhills.com

### CHATEAU MARMONT $$$ ❷ 3F

🕸 🍴 🍸 🛏 @ ☀ ❄ ℗

This faux French castle and its bungalows have long been a part of Hollywood's creative scene, and the place is the hotel of choice for writers, artists, and actors. 63 rooms, bungalows and suites. :: 8221 Sunset Blvd, West Hollywood, 323/656-1010, chateaumarmont.com

### FARMER'S DAUGHTER $$-$$$ ❷ 5F

🕸 🍴 🍸 🛏 @ ❄ ℗

Beautifully designed to be a more earthy, natural contrast to the plastic side of L.A., the cute country-styled rooms have gingham curtains and rocking chairs. Appropriately opposite the Farmers' Market, the hotel is also ideally located for trendy Third Street shopping (see p. 17) and restaurants. :: 115 S Fairfax Ave, Fairfax, 323/937-3930, 800/334-1658, farmersdaughter hotel.com

### HOLLYWOOD ROOSEVELT $$-$$$ ❷ 1A

🕸 🍴 🍸 🛏 @ ☀ ❄ ℗

This 1920s hotel was the original home of the Oscars, and is supposedly haunted by Marilyn Monroe. Its Tropicana bar is one of the latest places to see and be seen. Check out the poolside cabanas. :: 7000 Hollywood Boulevard, Hollywood, 323/466-7000, 800/950-7667, hollywoodroosevelt.com

### HOLLYWOOD STANDARD $$-$$$ ❷ 3F

🕸 🍴 🍸 🛏 @ ☀ ❄ ℗

The trendiest hotel on Sunset Strip offers a playful, minimalist interior with a lobby aquarium holding a human dummy instead of fish. The rooms are full of cacti and silver bean bags. The bar spills into the lobby and has nightly DJs; the party seems never-ending. A pool. :: 8300 Sunset Blvd, West Hollywood, 323/650-9090, standardhotel.com

## MAISON 140 $$ ❷ 5c

❖ ⅋ ♟ ♨ @ ☷ ☀ Ⓟ

This intimate 43-room hotel in a restored 1930s' colonial building with French and Mandarin-inspired interiors (blacks and reds), is high on style and close to Rodeo Drive and the big department stores along Wilshire Boulevard. ∷ 140 Lasky Dr, Beverly Hills, 310/281-4000, 800/670-6182, maison140beverlyhills.com

## MONDRIAN $$$-$$$$ ❷ 3e

❖ ⅋ ♟ ♨ @ ☷ ☀ Ⓟ

Ian Schrager's first Los Angeles hotel, this dreamy all-white high-rise is a favorite because of its large rooms, glass walls, diaphanous drapes, and famed Asia de Cuba restaurant, stylish pool (complete with the Skybar, drenched in celebrities). ∷ 8440 Sunset Blvd, West Hollywood, 323/650-8999, 800/697-1791 in the US, 00/800/4969-1780 internationally, mondrianhotel.com

## STANDARD DOWNTOWN $$-$$$ ❺

❖ ⅋ ♟ ♨ @ ☷ ☀ Ⓟ

The popular Rooftop Bar promises skyscraper views and waterbed pods. Inside, hotelier Andre Balazs' place is a shrine to 70s pop culture with bright fixtures and furnishings. Sister hotel to the Hollywood Standard (see p. 54). ∷ 550 South Flower St at 6th St, Downtown, 213/892-8080, standardhotel.com

## VALUE HOTELS

### NEW OTANI $$-$$$ ❺

❖ ⅋ ♟ ♨ @ ☷ ☀ Ⓟ

Located in Little Tokyo and every bit the Japanese experience, from the tatami mats to the tea service and massage. ∷ 120 S Los Angeles St, 213/629-1200, 800/639-6826, newotani.com

### RENAISSANCE HOLLYWOOD $$-$$$  2b

❖ ⅋ ♟ ♨ @ ☷ ☀ Ⓟ

At the Hollywood & Highland (see p. 18), with shopping and great restaurants at your fingertips. Also the venue of the Oscar after-show press coverage. ∷ 1755 N Highland Ave, Hollywood, 323/856-1200, 800/769-4774, marriott.com

## BUDGET HOTELS

### BEVERLY LAUREL MOTOR HOTEL $ ❷ 5f

⅋ ♨ ☀ Ⓟ

Inexpensive, but with attention to design detail. Rooms around a pool and next to Swingers (see p. 39). ∷ 8018 Beverly Blvd, 323/651-2441, 800/962-3824.

### FIGUEROA HOTEL $ ❺

⅋ ♟ ♨ ☀

This central hotel with a restaurant, bar, and pool, feels more luxurious than its prices might suggest. ∷ 939 S Figueroa St, Downtown, 213/627-8971, 800/421-9092, figueroahotel.com

### TRAVELODGE SANTA MONICA $ ❸

♔ ♟ ♨ ✳ ℗

This budget hotel is just across the street from Santa Monica Pier. :: 1525 Ocean Ave, Santa Monica 310/451-0761, 800/578-7878, travelodge.com

### VENICE BEACH COTEL $ ❸

♔ ♟ ♨ ✳

This value-for-money hostel is just back from the beach and Ocean Front Walk. Some rooms have private facilities and sea views. :: 25 Windward Ave, Venice, 310/399-7649, venicebeach cotel.com

## MUSEUMS

### CALIFORNIA HERITAGE MUSEUM ❸

This small museum showcases L.A life, past and present, with displays of decorative art and folk art. Each Sunday the museum hosts a farmers' market on the grounds. :: Adm. Open 11 am-4 pm Wed-Sun. 2612 Main St, Santa Monica, 310/392-8537, california heritagemuseum.org

### MUSEUM OF TOLERANCE ❷ 6D

Confronts racism and encourages harmony. :: Adm. Open 11:30 am-6:30pm Mon-Thu, 11 am-5 pm Fri, 11 am-7:30 pm Sun. 9786 W Pico Blvd, Century City, 310/553-8403, museumoftolerance.com

### MUSEUM OF TV & RADIO ❷ 5D

More than 90,000 TV programs—you can watch back episodes of *Lost* or *Desperate Housewives* in individual booths. :: Adm. Open 12 pm-5 pm Wed-Sun. 465 N Beverly Dr, 310/786-1025, mtr.org

### PETERSEN AUTOMOTIVE MUSEUM ❷ 6P

Dioramas celebrating the history of the American automobile, with a hands-on learning center for kids. :: Adm. Open 10 am-6 pm Tues-Sun. 6060 Wilshire Blvd, Westwood, 323/930-2277, petersen.org

### QUEEN MARY ❶ 5F

The grand old ocean liner shows off her luxurious first-class cabins and smaller steerage accommodations. The boat's restaurants are open later. :: Adm. Open 10 am-6 pm daily. Pier J, 1126 Queens Highway, Long Beach, 562/435-3511, queenmary.com

---

**HIDDEN EXTRAS**
Porters will expect $1 or $2 per bag. If there is valet parking, between 15 and 20 percent when you leave.

## PLACES OF INTEREST

### BERGAMOT STATION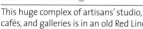

This huge complex of artisans' studio, cafés, and galleries is in an old Red Line station. :: 2525 Michigan Ave, Santa Monica, bergamotstation.com

### BRADBURY BUILDING 5

This elaborate Victorian building is one of L.A.'s few remaining wrought-iron structures to be still functioning as an office complex. :: Open 9 am-5 pm daily. 304 S Broadway, Downtown, 213/626-1893.

### CENTRAL LIBRARY 6

The splendid Art Deco building has a quiet garden. Stop by to see the California History Mural and the golden hand "Light of learning". :: Open 10 am-8 pm Mon-Thu, 10 am-6 pm Fri-Sat, 1 pm-5 pm Sun. 630 W 5th St, Downtown, 213/228-7000, lapl.org/central/

### HERITAGE SQUARE 1 2E

A living history museum covering the century between 1850 and 1950. :: Adm. Open noon-5 Fri-Sun. 3800 Homer St, Highland Park, 323/225-2900, heritagesquare.org

### HOLLYHOCK HOUSE 1 2E

This temple-like oddity was designed by Frank Lloyd Wright in 1921. :: Adm. Tours 12:30, 1:30, 2:30 & 3:30 pm Wed-Sun. Barnsdale Art Park, 4800 Hollywood Blvd, 323/644-6269, hollyhockhouse.net

### PASADENA MUSEUM OF HISTORY 4

Pasadena's history is displayed in the beautiful Beaux-Arts Fenyes Mansion. :: Adm. Open noon-5 pm Wed-Sun. 470 W Walnut St, Pasadena, 626/577-1660, pasadenahistory.org

### SKIRBALL CULTURAL CENTER 1 1C

Jewish cultural and arts center. Adm. :: Open noon-5 pm Tue-Fri, 11 am-5 pm weekdays. 2701 N Sepulveda Blvd, 310/440-4500, skirball.org

### SOUTH COAST BOTANIC GARDEN 1 5D

These stunning gardens are on top of a landfill site. Adm. :: Open 9 am-5 pm daily. 26300 Crenshaw Blvd, Palos Verdes, 310/544-6815, southcoast botanicgarden.org

### TOPANGA STATE PARK 1 2B

Hike the miles of trails that hook up to the Pacific Palisades or to the top of Bald Eagle Rock and view the entire sweep of Santa Monica Bay. :: Open 8 am to dusk. 20825 Entrada Rd, 310/455-2465, parks.ca.gov

### WATTS TOWERS ❶ 2E

These 99-ft cement towers are constructed from abandoned bedframes and pipes and mosaicked with glass, pottery and seashells. :: Open 10 am-4 pm Tues-Sat, noon-4 pm Sun. 1727 E 107th Street, 213/847-4646, parks.ca.gov

### WAYFARERS CHAPEL ❶ 5D

Pretty little glass-and-wood chapel. :: Open 8 am-5 pm daily. 5755 Palos Verdes Dr S, Rancho Palos Verdes, 310/377-1650, wayfarerschapel.org

### WILL ROGERS STATE HISTORIC PARK ❶ 2C

The former ranch of legendary actor, Will Rogers, with a 3-mile hiking trail. :: Adm. Park open 8 am-sunset daily. Guided tours of ranch Tues-Sun 11,1, and 2. 1501 Will Rogers State Pk Blvd, Pacific Palisades, 310/454-8212, parks.ca.gov/

## KIDS' VENUES

There's lots for kids to do in and around L.A. Don't forget Disneyland, Universal Studios, and Knott's Berry Farm.

### CABRILLO MARINE AQUARIUM ❶ 5E

♀♂ ♿ ▢ ▧

Sea life center with more than 30 aquariums and touch tanks for kids. :: Open noon-5 pm Tues-Fri, 10 am-5 pm Sat-Sun. 3720 Stephen M. White Dr, San Pedro, 310/548-7562, cabrilloaq.org

### KIDSPACE CHILDREN'S MUSEUM ❹

♀♂ ♿ ▢

A great museum with educational and creative exhibits. :: Adm. Open 9:30-5 daily. 480 N Arroyo Blvd, Pasadena, 626/449-9144, kidspacemuseum.org

## MEDIA LISTINGS

### LA WEEKLY

Weekly with extensive listings section. laweekly.com

## NEWSPAPERS

### LOS ANGELES TIMES

Daily paper read all over the state. latimes.com

## WEB SITES

**LA Convention and Visitors Bureau,** lacvb.com

**Los Angeles Cultural Calendar,** experiencela.com

**Los Angeles Magazine,** lamag.com

**Public Art In LA,** publicartinla.com

**Soul of America,** soulofamerica.com

**Time Out,** timeout.com

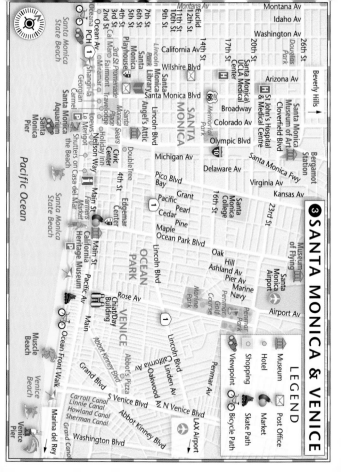

# ❸ SANTA MONICA & VENICE

## LEGEND

- ◉ Viewpoint
- Ⓟ Parking
- ⚡ Shopping
- ⚓ Skate Path
- ⛩ Market
- ⊘ Bicycle Path
- 🏛 Museum
- 🏨 Hotel
- ✉ Post Office

**Where® > CityGuide > Los Angeles**

Writing: Wendy Wheeler-Smith, Fiona Quinn
Other contributors: Cindy Boynton

Series design: Georgiana Goodwin
Page layout: Nancy Freeborn, Libby Kingsbury

Original PopOut maps design: CM Cartographics
Maps: Mary Ballachino

**Important Advice**

Always call ahead to make sure museums, sights, shops, and restaurants will be open when you show up. We've worked hard to make the text and maps accurate, but cities change fast, and it's better to be safe than sorry.

**Photo Credits**

All photographs by John Schoenfeld © Compass Maps, Ltd., except those on the following pages: Title page and page 2 © 2007 Jupiterimages Corporation. Page 6 courtesy of the Getty Museum. Page 11 courtesy of West Hollywood Convention and Visitors Bureau. Page 16 courtesy of Beverly Hills Convention and Visitors Bureau. Page 19t courtesy of Hollywood & Highland. Page 20r courtesy of the Farmers' Market. Page 23r courtesy of Flight 001. Pages 27tl, 29, and 44 by Robert Landau courtesy of LA Inc./LACVB. Page 52 © Charles Smith/Corbis. Also, from Shutterstock: 3t © Ivan Cholakov; 3m © Shannon West; 3b © Dan Breckwoldt; 9bl © David Alexander Liu; 14 © Ternovy Dmitry; 15t © Isaiah Shook; 15m and 27b © Silver-john; 15b © Radu Razvan; 24 © Elias H. Debbas II; 25t © Rafael Ramirez Lee; 25m © Mike Liu; 25b © Matt Purciel; 32tr © Bill Gruber; 33tr © Nikola Bilic; 34 © Thomas M Perkins; 35t © Xavier MARCHANT; 35m © Stasys Eidiejus; 41bl © Alin Popescu; 43tl © Roldolfo Arpia; 43bl © Kinetic Imagery; and 50 © Yusakn Takeda.

Library of Congress Cataloging-in-Publication Data on file
ISBN: 978-0-7627-4710-8

Printed in China
10 9 8 7 6 5 4 3 2 1

# Your Travel Portfolio™

Where® GuestBook™

Where® Magazine

Where® PopOut™
Maps & Guides

Where® QuickGuide™

Where® Maps

## Look for **where**® Travel publications in fine hotels and wherever books are sold.

Alaska & Yukon **Arizona** Atlanta **Baltimore** Boston **Budapest** Calgary
**Canadian Rockies** Charleston **Charlotte** Chicago **Colorado** Dallas **Edmonton**
Fort Worth **Georgia** Gold Coast **Greensboro Area** Halifax **Hawaii Big Island**
Hong Kong **Houston** Jacksonville **Kansas City** Kauai **Las Vegas** London
**Los Angeles** Macau **Maui** Miami **Milwaukee** Minneapolis/St. Paul **Mississauga**
Moscow **Muskoka/Parry Sound** New Orleans **New York** Northern Virginia **Oahu**
Orange County (CA) **Orlando** Ottawa **Paris** Philadelphia **Phoenix/Scottsdale**
Raleigh Durham Area **Rome** San Antonio **San Diego** San Francisco **Seattle**
Singapore **Southwest Florida** St. Louis **Tacoma** Tampa Bay Area **Tennessee**
Toronto **Tucson** Vancouver **Victoria** Washington, D.C. **Whistler** Winnipeg

## LEGEND

| | | | |
|---|---|---|---|
| 🛈 | Visitor Information | 📚 | Library |
| ○ | Place of Interest | 🅿 | Parking |
| 🏛 | Art Gallery/Museum | 🚌 | Bus Stop |
| 🎭 | Theater | 🎵 | Music Venue |
| ☐ | Shopping | 🎓 | University |
| ✉ | Post Office | Ⓜ | Metro |

The Rose Bowl
Gamble House
Pasadena Museum of History
Norton Simon Museum of Art
Pasadena Heritage
Tournament House & Wrigley Gardens
W California Blvd
S Orange Grove Blvd
Armory Ctr for the Arts
Memorial Park
Old Pasadena by Marriott
One Colorado
Westin
Pasadena Public Library
Fuller Theological Seminary
City Plaza
Hall
Pacific Asia Museum
Paseo Colorado
Pasadena Museum of California Art (PMCA)
Pasadena Conference & Exhibition Ctr/ Civic Auditorium
Sheraton
Hilton
Pasadena Playhouse
Pasadena Inn
Green Castle
Colorado Boulevard
Central Park
Dayton
Green
Del Mar
W Del Mar Blvd
De Lacey
S Pasadena
S Fair Oaks Av
S Raymond Av
Arroyo Pkwy
S Marengo Av
S Los Robles Av
S Euclid Av
S Oakland Av
S Madison Av
S El Molino Av
S Oak Knoll Av
S Hudson Av
Cordova
E Del Mar Blvd
The Shops on Lake Avenue
S Lake Av
Catalina Av
Colorado Blvd
E Colorado Blvd
E Union St
E Walnut St
Boston Court
Foothill Freeway
Lake
Westway Inn
Vagabond Inn
Saga Motor Hotel
Pasadena City College
E Green
E Michigan Av
Grant Park
N Chester Av
N Hollliston Av
N Hill Av
Rose Villa
Oakdale
San Pasqual
E Wilson Av
California Institute of Technology (Caltech)
Beckman Auditorium
Arden Rd
San Pasqual
E California Blvd
Cornell Rd
Oak Grove Av
Virginia Rd
Rosalind Rd
Avondale Rd
Tournament Park
SAN MARINO
Orlando Rd
Oxford Rd
Mausoleum
Botanical Center
Scott Galleries
Boone Gallery
Japanese House
The Huntington
Huntington Gallery
Botanical Gardens
Desert Gardens
Library
Orange Grove
Euston Rd
Lombardy Rd
S Sierra Bonita Av
S Bonnie Av
S Allen Av
E Del Mar Av
E California Blvd
S Meredith Av
S Parkwood Av
S Greenwood Av
Colorado Blvd
N Allen Av
LA County Arboretum, Santa Anita Park Racetrack
Ritz-Carlton Huntington Hotel
W Walnut
Maple
Colorado Blvd
Pasadena Park